Chaos and the creation
The beginning of time
17th century BCE
Babylonian
Epic of Atrahasis
Epic of Gilgamesh
12th century BCE
The Rig Veda
About 1500 BCE
About 750 BCE
Homer's Iliad and Odyssey
1184/3 BCE
Fall of Troy
1550–50 BCE
Egyptian
Book of Coming Forth by Day
Popol Vuh written down
1554–1558
Oral myths of Oceania recorded
19th & 20th centuries
About 1555
Journey to the West, attributed to Wu Cheng'en
1835
Finnish epic Kalevala by Elias Lönnrot
20th century
Indigenous American oral myths recorded
End of the world in the Maya calendar
21 December 2012
The future
The Apocalypse
20th & 21st centuries
African oral myths recorded
I0820955

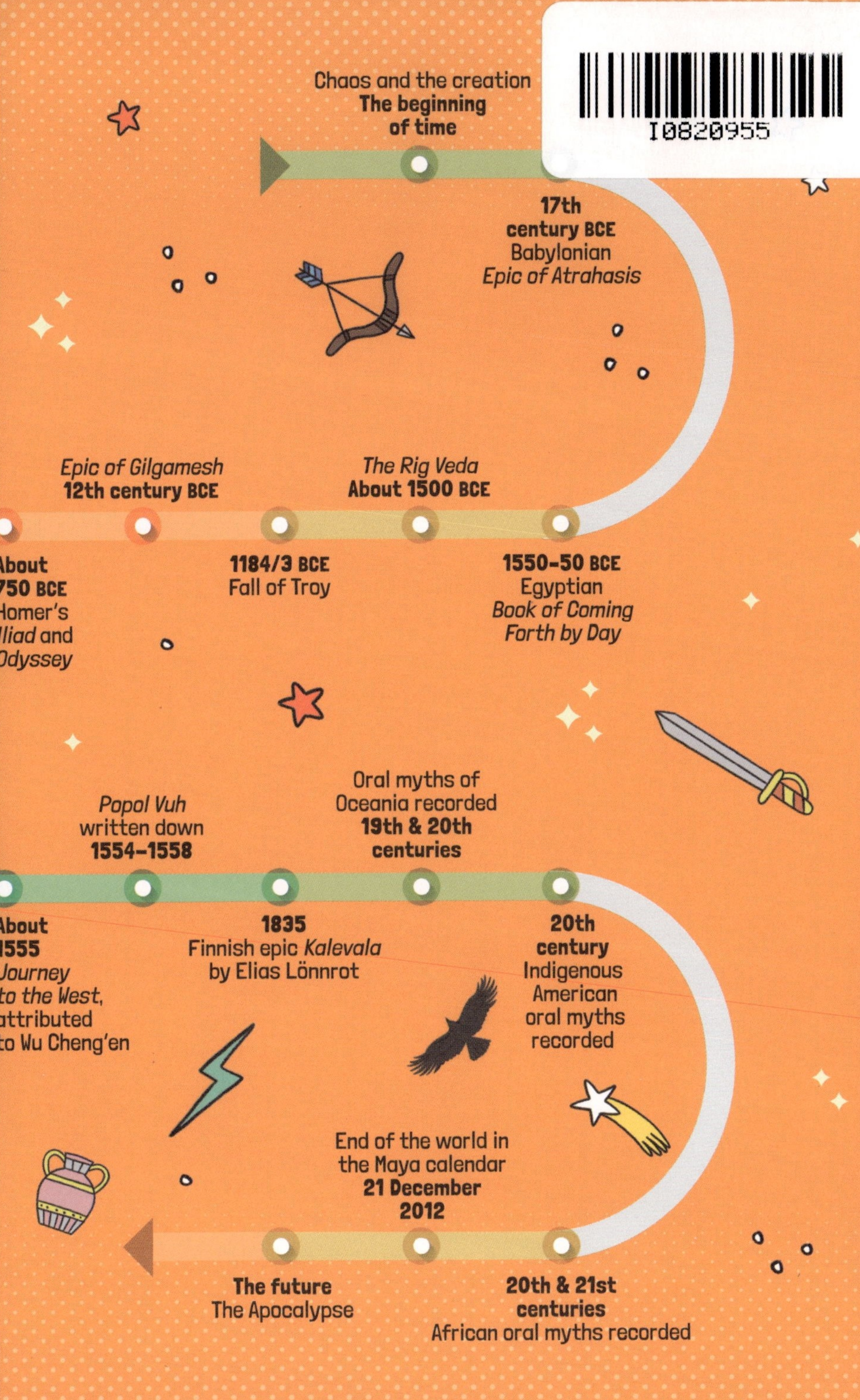

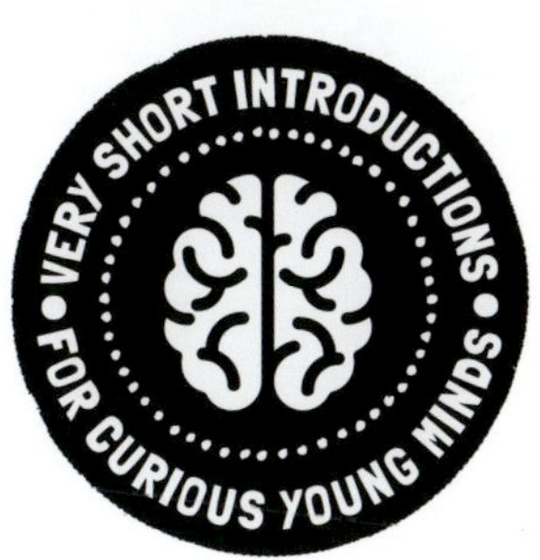

Ancient MYTHS, LEGENDS, and SUPERHEROES

Dr. Stephen Kershaw

OXFORD
UNIVERSITY PRESS

Great Clarendon Street, Oxford OX2 6DP

Oxford University Press is a department of the University of Oxford. It furthers the University's objective of excellence in research, scholarship, and education by publishing worldwide. Oxford is a registered trade mark of Oxford University Press in the UK and in certain other countries

Text written by Dr. Stephen Kershaw
Illustrated by Geraldine Sy and Ana Seixas

Designed and edited by Raspberry Books Ltd
The moral rights of the author and artist have been asserted

Database right Oxford University Press (maker)

First published 2023
This hardback edition published 2025

Library of Congress Cataloging-in-Publication

Data is available

ISBN: 978-1-382-07039-3

1 3 5 7 9 10 8 6 4 2

The manufacturing process conforms to the environmental regulations of the country of origin.

Printed in China

The manufacturer's authorised representative in the EU for product safety is Oxford University Press España S.A. of El Parque Empresarial San Fernando de Henares, Avenida de Castilla, 2 – 28830 Madrid (www.oup.es/en or product.safety@oup.com). OUP España S.A. also acts as importer into Spain of products made by the manufacturer.

Acknowledgments

The publisher and authors would like to thank the following for permission to use photographs and other copyright material:

Cover artwork: Geraldine Sy and Ana Seixas. Photos: Pavlo S/Shutterstock. **Inside photos:** p1: Pavlo S/Shutterstock; p14: MMCez/Shutterstock; pp28-29: notsuperstar/Shutterstock; p42: Pino Tage/Shutterstock; p52: Audrey Snider-Bell/Shutterstock; p60: Eric Isselee/Shutterstock; pp60-61: Roman Marusew/Shutterstock; p61: Sveta Aho/Shutterstock; p68: Mila_ls/Shutterstock; pp70-71: Hoika Mikhail/Shutterstock; p74(l): Drakuliren/Shutterstock; p74(r): Plateresca/Shutterstock; pp78-79: bluehand/Shutterstock; Jingjing Yan/Shutterstock; 42pixels/Shutterstock; pp82-83: Paolo Gallo/Shutterstock. **Front end paper:** pp2-3: Aleksandr Bryliaev/Shutterstock. **Back end paper:** p2: Pavlo S/Shutterstock.

Author photo courtesy of Dr. Steve Kershaw.

Artwork by **Geraldine Sy**, **Ana Seixas**, Ekaterina Gorelova, Adam Quest, Aaron Cushley, Raspberry Books, and Oxford University Press.

Every effort has been made to contact copyright holders of material reproduced in this book. Any omissions will be rectified in subsequent printings if notice is given to the publisher.

Contents

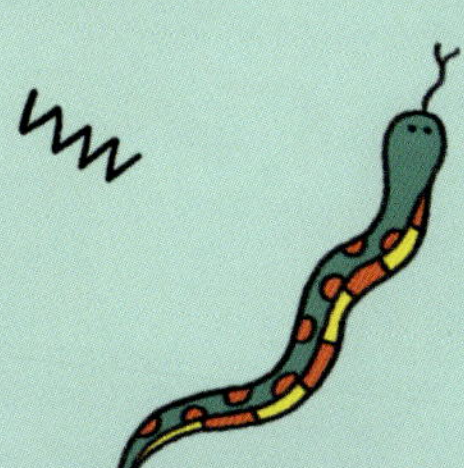
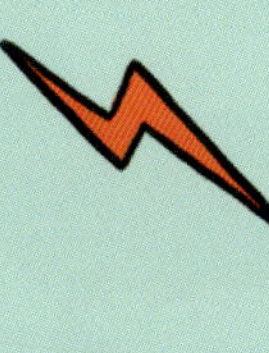

Myths and Legends Matter

People have been telling myths and legends featuring superhero superstars for thousands of years, and we are still reading them today.

Myths and legends are **fantastic stories** with **wondrous characters,** but there's much more to them than that. Humans tell myths because they help to make sense of what the world is like, how it works, where people came from, and why they live and think the way they do.

The stories are also full of **messages** that give us lots of important things to think about, although they don't always give us obvious answers. In the world of myths and legends even gods and heroes can behave badly, and people who make good choices don't always live happily ever after. With myths and legends, we need to **think for ourselves!**

Speak like a mythologist

MYTHOLOGIST

A mythologist is a person who studies legends, myths, and mythology. "Mythology" can mean a collection of stories, as in "tales from African mythology," or the study of those stories.

MYTH AND LEGEND

"Myth" comes from a Greek word, *mythos*. It means a story, or something you say. "Legend" comes from the Latin *legenda*, "things to be read." Myths can be hard to define, but most people agree that they are shared narratives that help to give a community a sense of identity, and create meaningful ways of understanding the world. Myths are very important to the members of the society they belong to, and they most often deal with subjects that relate to the **divine**, or the sacred.

Myths change all the time

Very often there are **several versions of the same story** told for different reasons by different people in different places at different times. A lot of tales were originally **passed around by word of mouth,** so they were always being retold and reworked. Once they were written down, they were preserved for generations to come, but even then people still told them in new ways. While a little book like this can't tell you about every version of every myth or legend, in this *Very Short Introduction to Myths, Legends, and Superheroes*, you will be introduced to some of the best known and most interesting ones.

The names of mythical characters come from many cultures and languages. This means there are many ways of spelling them. The Greek Akhilleus is known as Achilles in English, and some of the Greek gods and heroes are given Roman names too. Artemis is known as Diana, Zeus as Jupiter or Jove, and Odysseus as Ulysses.

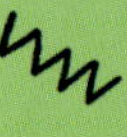

In this book, you'll discover why these **incredible stories** have stood the test of time and are still told all over the world.

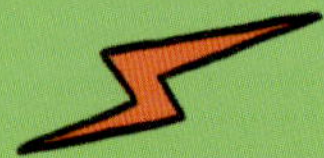

Find out about . . .

how a **spider** gained all the **wisdom** in the world

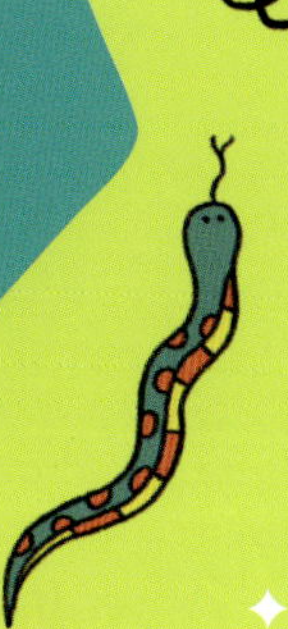

wolves that swallow the sun and moon

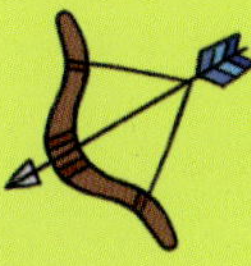

how to **travel through the mist** in a magical south-pointing chariot

the Lord and Lady of Death who **drank pus porridge** from skulls

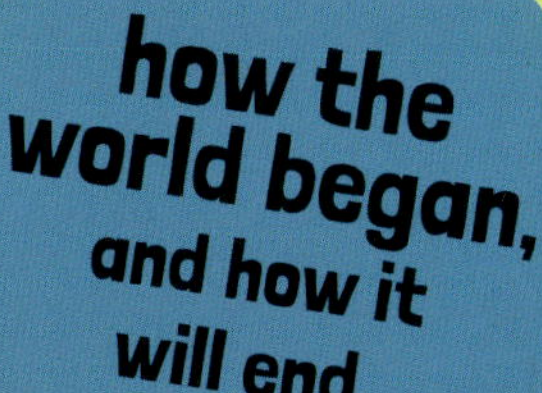

how the world began, and how it will end.

Read on, and be swept away by some of the **oldest, strangest,** and **most important** stories ever told.

Chapter 2

How the World Began

Where did the world come from? How? Why? People all over the world have their own creation stories that try to answer these big questions.

Everything comes from nothing

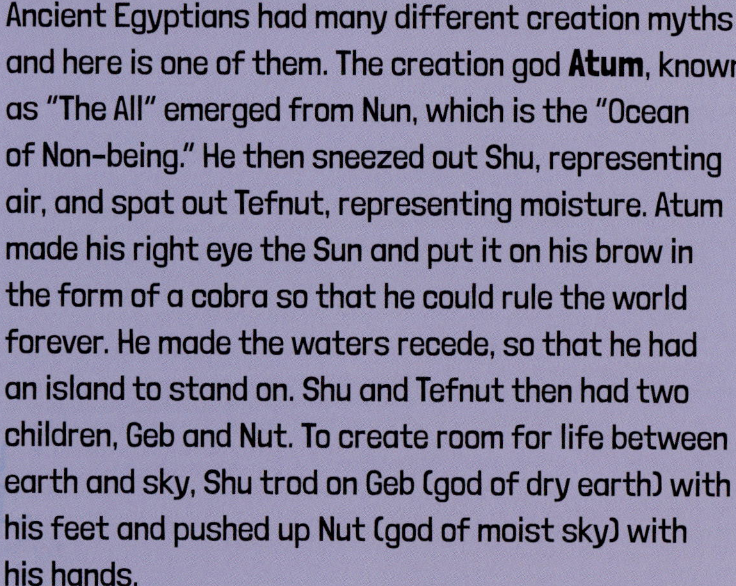

Ancient Egyptians had many different creation myths and here is one of them. The creation god **Atum**, known as "The All" emerged from Nun, which is the "Ocean of Non-being." He then sneezed out Shu, representing air, and spat out Tefnut, representing moisture. Atum made his right eye the Sun and put it on his brow in the form of a cobra so that he could rule the world forever. He made the waters recede, so that he had an island to stand on. Shu and Tefnut then had two children, Geb and Nut. To create room for life between earth and sky, Shu trod on Geb (god of dry earth) with his feet and pushed up Nut (god of moist sky) with his hands.

In the Jewish and Christian traditions, everything was dark until **Elohim,** also known as the Christian God, "the Supreme One," said: **"Let there be light."**

Then he made heaven, gathered the seas together, and made dry land appear. After plants and trees began to grow, he created the **Sun, Moon, and stars.** Finally, he populated the world with birds, sea monsters, fish, all kinds of land animals, and a man and a woman. This took him six days, and he rested on the seventh.

Atum, ancient Egyptian creation god

The **Islamic** tradition, recorded in the Qur'an and the sayings of the Prophet Mohammed known as the Hadith, follows a similar pattern. **Allah** said, **"Be,"** and created the world so that he might be known. It took Allah just **six days** to create the dark and the light, the heavens and the earth, the astral bodies, animals, and a man and a woman. He also created **hell** for those who choose to reject him as their god.

Many people believe these creation stories today. They give their god a capital letter and when they use the "his" pronoun, as a sign of respect.

Everything comes from chaos

In a poem called the *Theogony*, the ancient Greek poet Hesiod says that everything started with **Chaos**, which is the name of a god, but also describes a gaping, empty mess.

Then **Gaea**, goddess of the earth, emerged out of Chaos, along with the gloomy underground region of Tartarus and the love-god Eros.

Gaea

HEROES OF MYTH AND LEGEND

GAEA

(also known as Gaia or Ge)
The great mother goddess in ancient Greek mythology. She was parent of all living things, and granted humans children and fertile land.

Nyx, goddess of night, and Erebus, god of darkness, were then born from Chaos, and in their turn gave birth to Day and Bright Air. Next, Gaea created her partner Ouranos (Sky), the hills, and the sea-god Pontus, before giving birth to twelve more children. One of them, Cronus, badly wounded Ouranos using a mighty sickle, married his sister, Rhea, and became king of the gods. The Sun, Moon, stars, rivers, and winds all now appeared.

Because of a prophecy that Cronus would be dethroned by his own son, **he swallowed all his children at birth,** but when Rhea gave birth to Zeus, she disguised a stone as a baby and gave that to Cronus to swallow instead. So, Zeus grew up, overthrew his father and became king of the gods.

Speak like a mythologist

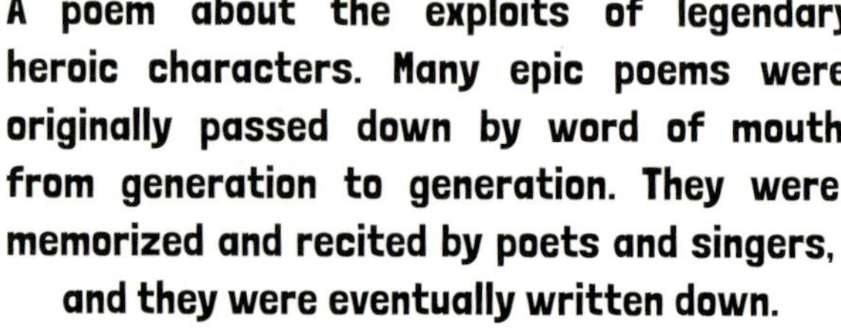

EPIC POEM

A poem about the exploits of legendary heroic characters. Many epic poems were originally passed down by word of mouth from generation to generation. They were memorized and recited by poets and singers, and they were eventually written down.

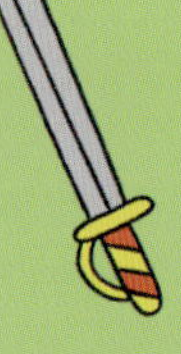

Everything comes from a dismembered body

One of the world's oldest creation stories is told in the Babylonian **epic** poem *Enuma Elish.* The poem, which was written in Ninevah, Iraq, in the language of Akkadian, is still preserved in clay tablets today.

In a time when even the sky and the earth had no names Apsu, god of Sweet Water, and Tiamat, goddess of Salt Water, **mingled their waters** and created the first gods. These new gods were so noisy that Apsu plotted to destroy them, but the wisest god, Ea, killed Apsu first.

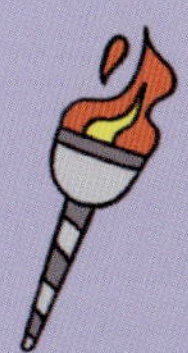

Tiamat wanted revenge. She created dragons, a horned serpent, a rabid dog, a scorpion-man, and other demons. The gods were terrified, but Ea's son Marduk fought back, killed Tiamat, and created the world **by slicing Tiamat's body in two.** One half of her made the heavens, the other made the earth. Marduk used Tiamat's eyes to make the Tigris and Euphrates rivers, and created the city of **Babylon** to be the home of the gods. Human beings were created from the blood of Tiamat's lover Qingu, so that the gods could have servants.

Tiamat

Marduk

Earth-diving and cosmic eggs

Right across the world there are tales of how a creator sent an **"earth-diver"** into the primal waters to bring up little bits of mud and sand, which gradually formed dry land. In the oral tradition of the Ainu people of Japan, one variant of the creation story says that the earth-diver was a type of bird called a water wagtail.

a water wagtail

It used its wings to splash the waters and reveal little patches of ground, which it packed down using its feet and tail to form the islands where the Ainu live.

In other creation stories, everything emerged from a cosmic egg. A story from Tahiti tells of a massive egg-shaped shell floating in nothingness at the dawn of time. The feathered god Ta'aroa lived inside the egg until he decided to crack it open and create life.

He pushed up half of the broken shell to form the **heavens** and used the bottom half to make the **earth.**

Then Ta'aroa made soil from his own skin, clouds from his insides, oceans, lakes, and rivers from his tears, mountain ranges from his bones, trees from his feathers, sea creatures from his guts, and the colors of the sky and rainbows from his blood. Finally, he created children who hung the Sun, Moon, and stars in the sky, and helped to make more plants and animals. Ta'aroa then made the first people.

Ta'aroa

These creation stories are **how people from various cultures explained how the world began.** In the next chapter we can explore some intriguing tales that tell us how the gods made human beings.

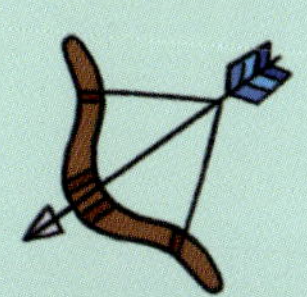

Chapter 3

Where Did Human Beings Come From?

How were we made? Did human beings evolve? Were we created? Who or what created us? Across the world there are extraordinary stories that give mythical answers to the origin of life.

Askr and Embla

A lot of what we know about **Norse** mythology comes from the ***Poetic Edda*** and the ***Prose Edda.*** In the *Prose Edda*, the god Odin was strolling along the beach with his brothers Vili and Ve. They found two pieces of driftwood and shaped a man and woman from them. They named the woman **Embla** ("Elm" or "Vine") and the man **Askr** ("Ash Tree"). Askr and Embla were given Midgard ("Middle World") at the base of a mighty ash tree called Yggdrasil, which grew right in the middle of the cosmos and held the eight Norse worlds together. There, Embla gave birth to the first humans. The gods then **created their own world of Asgard** in the sky and joined it to Midgard with a fiery Rainbow Bridge

called **Bifrost,** which humans often see, but only the gods could cross.

Yggdrasil, the ash tree that held the eight Norse worlds together

Asgard

Alvheim

Vanaheim

Bifrost

Svartalvheim

Muspelheim

Midgard

Nivlheim

Jotunheim

Hel (the underworld)

The Popol Vuh story of the K'iche' Maya

The *Popol Vuh* (meaning "Book of Advice") of the **K'iche' Maya** people from Guatemala was passed on by word of mouth until it was written down in around **1550 CE.** It told how the gods wanted to be remembered, but the animals couldn't say their names. So, **Tz'aqol** and **B'itol,** along with **Xmucane** and **Xpiyacoc,** created a human out of soil from the earth. Unfortunately, it went all mushy and dissolved when it got wet.

The gods made a second version out of wood. These creatures looked and talked like humans, but they had no blood, no sweat, and no souls, and did not remember their creators. Then, the god **Huracan** sent down a Great Flood, and the wooden people were attacked by Chiselers of Faces, Death Knives, jaguars, dogs, cooking pots, and tortilla grinders.

The gods succeeded on their third attempt. They discovered maize, and created four humans from that. These people had wisdom and understanding, could see through mountains and seas, and respected the gods. But the humans were **too godlike,** so the gods tweaked them, making sure they couldn't become divine. The gods gave the people partners, and the people's hearts were filled with joy. They had children, planted crops, and praised the gods.

Speak like a mythologist

PATRIARCHY

Most ancient societies were patriarchies. This means men had the power. In many creation stories the men were made first, and then the women to be their companions and helpers. The men didn't want to share their power, so they often invented myths in which women caused trouble for everyone, whether accidentally or on purpose. As you read the stories in this book, think about how they reflect these patriarchal societies and their beliefs.

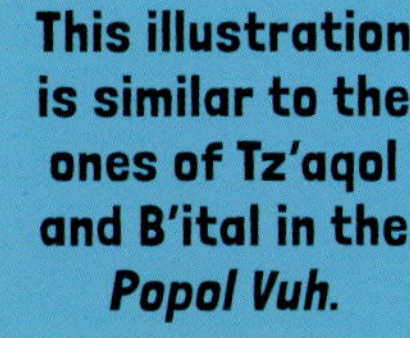

This illustration is similar to the ones of Tz'aqol and B'ital in the *Popol Vuh*.

Adam and Eve

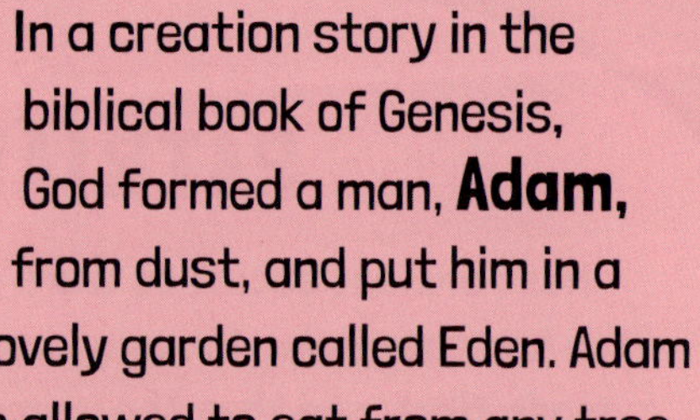

In a creation story in the biblical book of Genesis, God formed a man, **Adam,** from dust, and put him in a lovely garden called Eden. Adam was allowed to eat from any tree except the Tree of the Knowledge of Good and Evil. God used one of Adam's ribs to make a woman, **Eve.**

Unfortunately, there was a **sly serpent** in the garden who told Eve that if she ate the forbidden fruit, she would gain knowledge of good and evil. Eve wanted to gain wisdom, so she **ate some fruit,** and gave some to Adam. They instantly realized they were naked, covered themselves up with fig leaves, and tried to hide from God. God told the couple that their lives would now be full of hard work and pain, and banished them from the Garden of Eden.

Eve means "living" because she would become the mother of all living people.

Abuk and Garang

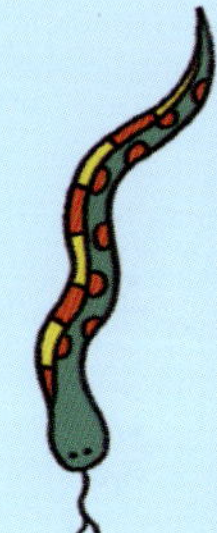

The Dinka people of South Sudan tell of **Abuk,** the first woman, and **Garang,** the first man. The creator god Nhialic molded them out of clay and put them in a large pot where they grew into human beings.

Nhialic gave them one seed of grain a day to eat, but they were hungry, so Abuk decided to eat one grain on alternate days, plant the other one, and grow her own crops. Nhialac wasn't happy about this. He cut the rope that tied the earth to his heavenly home, and from that moment humans have **had to experience work, sickness, and death.** Despite being the one who upset the creator, Abuk is still celebrated by the Dinka people.

Pandora

In **Greek mythology**, Prometheus, whose name means "Foresight," stole fire from Zeus and gave it to men. But Zeus hated being cheated, and ordered the creation of the first woman, Pandora. **Pandora was loved by everyone,** but she was also a cunning liar.

Zeus introduced Pandora to Prometheus's brother Epimetheus ("Hindsight"), along with a gift of a **large jar** that contained all the world's troubles. Epimetheus forgot he'd been told never to accept any gifts from Zeus, and now it was too late: Pandora opened the jar and **the troubles escaped,** leaving only Hope still trapped inside when she **slammed** the lid shut. Is there now no hope, because Hope is shut in the jar? Or do we at least have hope, if nothing else?

Pandora

Speak like a mythologist

PANDORA'S BOX

The modern expression "to open a Pandora's box" means to do something that will cause lots of problems that you haven't thought about. In the original story, Pandora didn't have a box. She had a jar called a *pithos* in Greek, but a sixteenth-century scholar called Erasmus made a mistake when he was doing a translation, and her container has been called a box ever since.

The world was a much more interesting place with human beings in it. But the gods didn't necessarily love the humans, and the humans would often try to trick the gods as they worked out how to deal with all the challenges that life brought them.

In the next chapter, we will explore the rich stories of some of the **most amazing humans** who lived in this world of myth and legend.

Chapter 4

Superheroes

Today's superheroes, such as Batman, Power Girl, Superman, and Wonder Woman, have extraordinary powers. They are inspired by ancient heroes' miraculous births, magical weapons, and brilliant skills. Superheroes can also be complex characters who show strength and loyalty, and can excite fear, love, and pity.

RHIANNON

Cunning hero Rhiannon features in the *Mabinogion*, a collection of Welsh myths.

When Prince Pwyll saw and fell in love with Rhiannon riding her magical white horse, his men tried and failed to catch up with her. Only when Pwyll asked

Rhiannon on her magical white horse

her to stop did she wait for him. Rhiannon declared that she was betrothed to Gwawl but would rather marry Pwyll. The prince was delighted.

But at a grand feast, Gwawl turned up in disguise and tricked Pwyll into giving up Rhiannon. Rhiannon came up with a clever plan. She gave Pwyll a magic bag and told him to arrange another feast in Gwawl's honor. Pwyll disguised himself and asked to fill his bag with food. Gwawl agreed, but no matter how much food was put into the bag, it never filled up. Rhiannon encouraged Gwawl to stamp the food down and when he stood in the bag, Pwyll pulled it shut and tied it closed.

Rhiannon instructed Pwyll to release Gwawl from the bag on the condition that he agreed not to seek revenge, and Pwyll and Rhiannon were finally united.

Speak like a mythologist

THE *MABINOGION*

A collection of eleven medieval Welsh tales, full of heroic and supernatural elements, about the legendary past of the British Isles. Based on the spoken tradition of storytelling, they are preserved in written form in the *White Book of Rhydderch* (1300–1325) and the *Red Book of Hergest* (1375–1425).

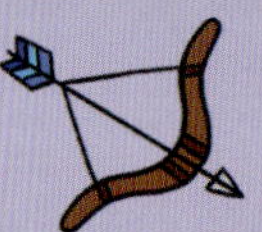

Mami Wata

Mami Wata ("Mother Water") is an unpredictable figure who can be mysterious, protective, and dangerous all at the same time. The legend originated in Africa between the sixteenth and nineteenth centuries and was spread to the Americas by enslaved African people who valued her strength and support. Mami Wata is celebrated today in over twenty African countries, as well as the African **diaspora**.

Mami Wata

Mami Wata is often like a **mermaid**. She has the upper half of a woman and lower half of a fish, and she often carries a snake. She is a nurturing figure who looks after people's physical, spiritual, and mental health, and many who respect her are healers or leaders.

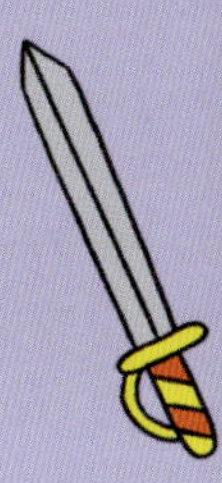

Mami Wata can bring good or bad fortune in the form of money, which can be a blessing or a curse, and her followers are both attracted to and scared by all the hopes, fears, risks, and rewards that she can bring.

Louhi and her daughter

Shape-shifting Louhi was the ruler of the northern land of Pohjola in the Finnish epic poem the *Kalevala.* The first man, Väinämöinen, set out from Kalevala to marry Louhi's daughter. Louhi would only agree if Väinämöinen got the blacksmith Ilmarinen to make the *sampo*—a mysterious tool that could grind flour, make salt, and create gold out of thin air.

We never learn the name of Louhi's daughter, but she too gave tasks to Väinämöinen, including building a boat from the splinters of a spindle. He failed her tasks but Ilmarinen did forge the *sampo* out of white swan feathers, the milk of virtue, one grain of barley, and the finest lambswool. Ilmarinen gave the *sampo* to Louhi, who hid it under a hill in Pohjola.

Some time later, Väinämöinen sailed to Pohjola to steal the *sampo.* He used the jaw of a massive fish to make the *kantele,* a magic **zither** that sent everyone to sleep while he sailed off with the *sampo.* Louhi woke up, turned into a giant eagle, and swooped after him . . . but as they fought, the *sampo* fell into the sea.

Louhi was furious: She sent nine plagues against the people of Kalevala, but Väinämöinen cured them all. When she sent a bear to **attack** their cattle, Väinämöinen defeated it. Louhi confiscated fire, but Väinämöinen caught a fire-fish and got it back. Then she hid the Sun and the Moon in iron-banded caves, but Väinämöinen made her put them back in the sky. So the world went back to how it was.

Speak like a mythologist

THE *KALEVALA*

The *Kalevala* ("Land of Heroes") is an epic poem first told orally. It was written down from old Finnish songs and poems by a doctor called Elias Lönnrot in the nineteenth century.

Antigone (*pronounced* An-**ti**-guh-nee)

In Greek mythology it is sometimes necessary to make **impossible** choices. In a tragic play by Sophocles, written in around **441 BCE**, Antigone's brothers, Eteocles and Polynices, had both died fighting each other over who should become king of **Thebes.** Antigone's uncle Creon, now the king, decreed that Polynices' corpse should be left to rot and that anyone trying to bury him should be put to death.

What should Antigone do? **Ignore her duty to bury her beloved brother, or disobey the king?**

She respected the laws of the gods more than the laws of humans, so gave Polynices the traditional funeral rites. Creon decreed that she should be entombed alive, but then changed his mind. By then, though, Antigone had ended her own life. Creon's son Haemon, who was in love with Antigone, was so distraught he also ended his life. Creon's **heartbroken** wife Eurydice died by suicide too, laying terrible curses on the devastated king.

an Amazon warrior

Her story inspired the English playwright Shakespeare and the French playwright Anouilh to write powerful plays about her.

The Amazons

In Greek and Roman stories the ultimate mythological powerful women were the Amazons, athletic and colorfully dressed warriors. The Amazons were challengers of men and could fight at long-range with their bows and arrows, or at close quarters with their spears and shields. They gave away male babies and only brought up the females. They also removed their right breasts to stop them getting in the way when they threw their javelins. These legendary women were the inspiration for **Wonder Woman** in DC Comics, who was sculpted from clay by her Amazon mother Hippolyta and given superhuman powers by the Greek gods.

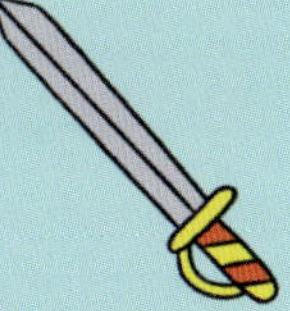

Speak like a mythologist

HERO

"Hero" is derived from the Greek word *heros*. A modern real-life hero is usually someone who is respected for doing or achieving great or brave things. A mythological hero is someone who often has a divine parent and superhuman powers, but is still very much like us. Heroes suffer the joys and pain of human life, can be wise or foolish, and can do both good and bad things.

The Twelve Labors of Heracles

The **mightiest Greek hero** was Heracles. He's most famous for completing twelve impossible-sounding Labors, though there are different versions of the myth. One story says that the goddess Hera hated him, and made him kill his family. To make amends, Heracles had to complete twelve tasks set by his enemy, King Eurystheus. **And they were very hard tasks . . .**

1 Kill the Nemean Lion.

Weapons can't pierce the lion's skin.

2 Kill the Lernaean Hydra.

the Hydra

3 Capture the Ceryneian Hind.

golden antlers

bronze hooves

4 Catch the Erymanthian Boar.

5 Clean the Augean Stables.

Heracles diverted the course of two rivers to clean the stables.

6 Drive away the Stymphalian Birds.

bronze beaks

can shoot feathers like arrows

10

Capture Geryon's cattle.

Geryon

Speak like a mythologist

Heracles means "Hera's Glory" in Greek, but people most often use the Roman form, which is Hercules. Which one is correct? They both are!

As the favored son of Zeus, Heracles became a god after his death.

Cúchulainn

The Irish Cúchulainn was the son of the god Lugh and the mortal Deichtine. He got his name when, as a child, he killed the blacksmith Culann's guard dog, but promised to take its place as the "Hound of Culann," which is what Cúchulainn means in Irish.

When Cúchulainn was seven years old he heard a **druid** prophesy that anyone who picked up weapons and got ready to fight that day would have eternal fame. So, Cúchulainn asked his uncle Conchobar of Ulster for his weapons. But he had not heard the rest of the prophecy: The warrior would live a very short life, just like Achilles, who we will meet later on.

Aged seventeen, Cúchulainn fought against Queen Mebd of Connaught, who wanted to steal the Brown Bull of Cooley. He slaughtered Mebd's troops with the deadly Gae-Bolg ("Spear of Mortal Pain"), but of course he could not escape the druid's prophecy. Shortly after the battle, Cúchulainn himself was fatally wounded by a magical spear. He tied himself to a stone so that he would die standing up.

Sigurd

When a hoard of gold, including a cursed ring, was stolen by the venomous dragon-serpent Fafnir, Norse hero Sigurd swore to kill the thieving monster.

He hid in a trench near the beast's lair and, as Fafnir slithered over it, he thrust his sword into the serpent's belly and killed it. But the curse of the ring passed on to Sigurd as he took the treasure.

The curse of the ring came true when Sigurd was traveling some time later. He awakened the **Valkyrie**

Brynhildr from a sleeping spell and promised to marry her, but then drank a potion of forgetfulness and married the princess Gudrun instead. Gudrun's brother married Brynhildr and killed Sigurd, then Brynhildr ended her own life.

Sigurd in battle with Fafnir

Speak like a mythologist

THE *VÖLSUNGA SAGA*

The *Völsunga Saga* is a thirteenth century poem written in the Old Norse language. It tells of the rise and fall of the Völsung clan, who were descended from the god Odin. Sigurd is the main character in the story.

MAGIC RINGS

Sigurd's story inspired the composer Richard Wagner's mighty opera *The Ring of the Nibelung* and J. R. R. Tolkein's *The Lord of the Rings*. Magic rings also appear in Harry Potter's world.

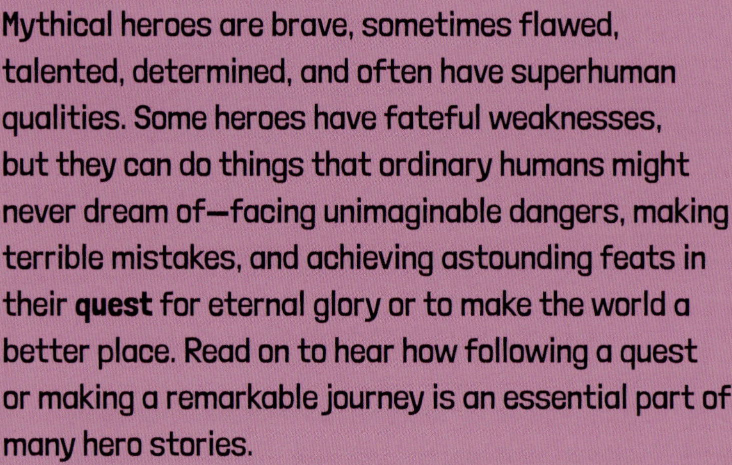

Mythical heroes are brave, sometimes flawed, talented, determined, and often have superhuman qualities. Some heroes have fateful weaknesses, but they can do things that ordinary humans might never dream of—facing unimaginable dangers, making terrible mistakes, and achieving astounding feats in their **quest** for eternal glory or to make the world a better place. Read on to hear how following a quest or making a remarkable journey is an essential part of many hero stories.

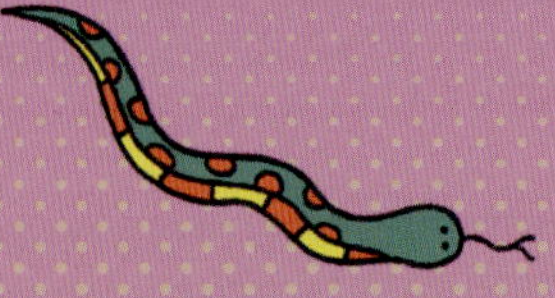

Chapter 5

Mythical Journeys and Quests

Awesome journeys and quests appear in the myths and legends of nearly every people in the world.

Stories like this, where the hero heads off, encounters fabulous forces, and wins a wonderful victory, are often called "the Hero's Journey." We see these story patterns in *Star Wars, Toy Story, Frozen, Harry Potter, The Hunger Games, The Lord of the Rings*, and countless other tales, as well as in ancient legends.

Speak like a mythologist

THE HERO'S JOURNEY

There are patterns in many hero stories. When the adventure starts, the heroes might need someone to help them begin their journey. They meet friends and enemies, and, as they approach their goal, they have to face a big test. When it looks like they will succeed, they must deal with even more problems. Finally they return home in triumph, having learned things and matured during their journey.

The *Odyssey*

On his **amazing** voyage home to Ithaca after the **Trojan War**, the cunning Greek hero Odysseus had to face all sorts of incredible challenges. It took him **ten years,** but he made it home in the end.

The Laestrygonians were cannibal giants.

He sailed past the dangerous, magical singing Sirens.

Odysseus spent a year on the enchantress Circe's island.

Circe

ITALY

Odysseus escaped from the sea monster Scylla and the whirlpool of Charybdis.

Odysseus met a Cyclops and blinded him with a sharp wooden stake.

SICILY

The nymph Calypso's island—Odysseus spent seven years there!

TUNISIA

The land of the Lotus-eaters. Anyone who ate the fruit of the lotus would never leave!

This map of Greece and parts of Turkey, Italy, and Tunisia charts where some of Odysseus's **fictional voyages** might be in the real world—though many of the lands in the story aren't on any actual map.

Speak like a mythologist

THE *ODYSSEY*

The *Odyssey* is a Greek epic poem that tells of the hero Odysseus's ten-year journey home after the Trojan War. "Odyssey" has become the word for a long trip full of different and exciting adventures.

HOMER

The name given to the author of two Greek poems, the *Iliad* and the *Odyssey*, which had been memorized and repeated for hundreds of years before they were written down in around 750 BCE. It is a mystery who Homer was, where he came from, whether he wrote both poems, or whether each poem was created by just one person. But the poems are still being read and studied today.

Sindbad the Sailor

The *Odyssey* inspired the adventures of Sindbad the Sailor in a collection of stories known as the *Thousand and One Nights* or *The Arabian Nights*, which was written down in Arabic in the fifteenth century.

Sindbad was a merchant from Baghdad who made **seven fantastic journeys** that made him very rich. On his first voyage, he landed on an island that was actually a whale and was almost drowned when it dove into the sea. On his second trip, Sindbad used a **huge** mythical bird called a Roc to help him collect diamonds.

Sindbad and the Roc

Sindbad's next adventures remind us of Odysseus. He met a Cyclops-like giant who ate several of his sailors before he blinded it with red-hot iron spits. Like Odysseus with the Laestrygonians, during his fourth trip, Sindbad was shipwrecked among cannibals, but **again he escaped.**

On Sindbad's other adventures he survived being buried alive, attacked by more Rocs, shipwrecked, and captured by the Old Man of the Sea. His final voyage took him to the farthest corner of the world, where the local people turned into birds and Sindbad flew above the clouds on one of them. These bird-people were in fact devils, but when Sindbad praised Allah, they dropped him on a mountaintop. He returned home, and never went to sea again.

Xuanzang, Sun Wukong, and the "Journey to the West"

The sixteenth-century Chinese novel *Journey to the West* by Wu Cheng'en is inspired by myth and legend and features a clever trickster, the Monkey King Sun Wukong, who was born from a magic stone egg.

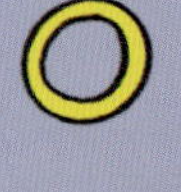

When one of Sun Wukong's friends died, he decided he wanted to cheat death. He went to the great teacher Master Puti to learn how to be immortal, as well as some other awesome supernatural skills like shape-shifting and

somersaulting over clouds. When Sun Wukong got home, he stole the Dragon King's magic weapon, fought off the ambassadors from hell, and rubbed his own name off the *Register of the Living and the Dead.* This made him immortal.

The supreme god, The Great Yu, decreed that Sun Wukong should be moved to heaven, where he could keep an eye on him. But Sun Wukong caused havoc there, and even ate the Peaches of Immortality that belonged to the Heavenly Queen Mother.

So, Sun Wukong was imprisoned underneath a mountain until, 500 years later, Guanyin, the goddess of mercy, had him released on the condition that he went to India with a monk called Xuanzang on a quest to fetch some sacred *sutras*—teachings of the **Buddha**.

After eighty-one adventures among demons, evil wizards, raging rivers, and uncontrollable monsters, Xuanzang and Sun Wukong got the sutras from the Buddha himself. Sun Wukong was rewarded with the title "Victorious Fighting Buddha."

HEROES OF MYTH AND LEGEND

WU CHENG'EN

A writer of the Chinese Ming Dynasty in the sixteenth century. His writing was inspired by myth and folklore, though *Journey to the West* was based on a real trip to India made by the monk Xuanzang in the seventh century.

On their journeys and quests, heroes often have to face **terrifying** creatures if they are to make it safely home. So let's meet some of the scariest creatures, and discover how to deal with them.

Chapter 6

Monsters and Monster-Slayers

Myths and legends are crammed with fire-breathing, snaky, flesh-eating, turn-you-to-stone creatures. Others are harmless, but people still fight against them.

Medusa

Medusa was one of the three Gorgons. Anyone who looked at her turned to stone.

The Greek hero Perseus was given the seemingly impossible task of bringing back Medusa's head. So, he set off armed with a pair of winged sandals, a special bag, the cap of invisibility, and a sickle made of adamant, the hardest metal in myth. To avoid looking at Medusa directly, he used a bronze shield to reflect her image while he chopped off her head. Then he stuffed it into his bag, put on the cap of invisibility, and flew away.

Speak like a mythologist

APOTROPAIC

The Greeks and Romans often hung carvings of Medusa's head on buildings. These were believed to be "apotropaic," meaning they could avert evil forces and keep bad luck away.

The Minotaur

The Minotaur, which means **"Bull of Minos,"** was thought of as a monster. People were scared of someone who looked so different, with the body of a human and the head and tail of a bull. The Minotaur was named after King Minos of Crete, who was so horrified

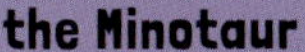

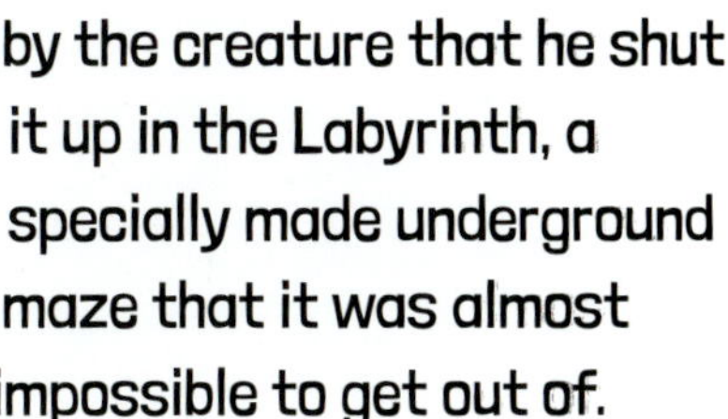

by the creature that he shut it up in the Labyrinth, a specially made underground maze that it was almost impossible to get out of.

Minos also forced the king of Athens to send a tax of seven young men and seven young women every year as food for the Minotaur. One year, the king's son, Theseus, was chosen to be one of these "Minotaur victims." Theseus intended to terminate both the Minotaur and the tax. When he arrived in Crete, Minos's daughter Ariadne **fell in love with Theseus.**

Ariadne gave Theseus a **ball of thread** to unwind as he went down into the Labyrinth, where he and the Minotaur fought to the death. Theseus won and used the thread to find his way out again.

HEROES OF MYTH AND LEGEND

THESEUS

Ancient Greek minotaur-slaying hero.

The Qallupilluit

The Inuit who live in the Arctic regions of Alaska, Canada, Siberia, and Greenland tell stories of the terrifying Qallupilluit. The Qallupilluit are human-shaped creatures that live in the icy waters where the land meets the sea. They have green, slimy, scaly skin, with claw-like fingernails, and long hair. They lure young children

a Qallupilluit

onto thin ice and snatch them when it breaks, then carry their victims away in a pouch. Inuit adults tell these scary stories to make sure that children don't wander off on their own onto the dangerous ice.

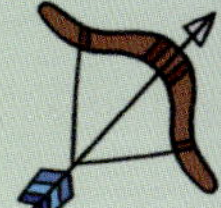

HEROES OF MYTH AND LEGEND

EDWARD W. NELSON

An early American ethnographer who collected information about Inuit myths and folktales. An ethnographer is a person who studies different cultures, often using first-hand observation and interviews.

Kut-o-yis

Some heroes sacrifice themselves to overcome evil beings. The **Indigenous American Blackfoot Nation** have a hero called Kut-o-yis.

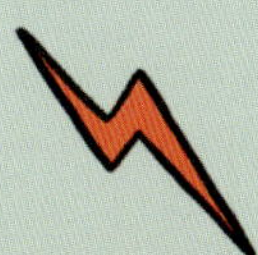
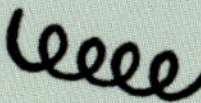

An old man stole a big clot of blood from the carcass of a buffalo that he and his stingy son-in-law had hunted. The son-in-law never allowed him any meat from their hunting, so the old man and his wife **boiled the blood clot** in a pot to make soup. They were amazed to hear a noise like a child in pain, so they opened the lid and found a little boy. They named him Kut-o-yis, "Blood-clot Boy", but told their daughters the baby was a girl.

After just four days Kut-o-yis had grown into an adult. He took revenge on the son-in-law for being so mean to the old man, before heading off to kill all the bad things in the world.

He dispatched a rattlesnake, and then went into the mouth of the people-swallowing Wind Sucker, stabbed

it in the heart, and freed everyone inside. After defeating two women who terrorized travelers, Kut-o-yis came to the **great Man-Eater**. He allowed the monster to kill, cook, and eat him four times, but every time Kut-o-yis was reborn, and he finally killed the Man-Eater by throwing it into its own cooking pot.

Beowulf and Grendel

Beowulf is the hero of an **Anglo-Saxon** poem. He went to Denmark to help King Hrothgar fight the

giant demon Grendel.

Grendel was a "shadow-walker," a cursed descendant of Cain, the first murderer in the Christian **Bible**. Grendel hated the joyful sounds that came from Hrothgar's feasting hall, and every night he terrorized the partying Danes.

But when Grendel tried to devour Beowulf, the unarmed hero ripped off the demon's arm, and Grendel ran away and died in his marshy lair.

In his relentless fight against evil creatures, Beowulf also fought a brutal battle with Grendel's vengeful mother, slaying her with an ancient sword he found in her underwater hall. After that, Beowulf had to confront a **fire-breathing** dragon that was ravaging his kingdom of **Geatland**.

He entered its den and killed it, but not before it had sunk its fangs into his throat. And so Beowulf died, fighting to save his own people.

Beowulf

Speak like a mythologist

BEOWULF

The hero of a poem of the same name that was written in Old English somewhere between 975 and 1025 CE, although we don't know who wrote it. *Beowulf* is 3,182 lines long and there is only one copy of it, in the British Library in London, UK.

Caipora: guardian of the rainforest

Tales from the South American **Tupí-Guaraní** peoples' mythology were first written down in the sixteenth century. A popular character is the Caipora, whose name means "forest inhabitant." The Caipora is described in many different ways by the separate peoples.

The Caipora often appears as a small human-shaped creature with a long mane of flame-colored hair and red eyes, riding on a **peccary** and shaking a short spear.

This is one interpretation of what the Caipora could look like.

All the stories agree that the Caipora is as ***fast as a gust of wind***, and that it protects the forests and animals. If hunters do not respect the rules of fair play, it whips them or confuses them, makes them have bad luck, and gets them lost in the jungle. The Caipora imitates animal noises, leaves false tracks, scares off the hunters' prey, and can even bring animals back to life.

The Caipora has inspired modern writers too. In the world of Harry Potter, the Caipora are mischievous, furry spirit-beings who protect the Wizarding Castle of Castelobruxo in the Brazilian jungle. In DC Comics, Caipora is a companion of the second Wonder Woman, Yara Flor, and is a guardian of the Amazon rainforest.

If you are going to deal with a mythical creature, you will need **strength** and **courage**, and possibly a **magic weapon** and help from your companions. But even this might not be enough. You will need to be cunning and crafty, and some of the most entertaining legendary characters are clever tricksters, as we will see . . .

Chapter 7

Trickery and Shape-Changing

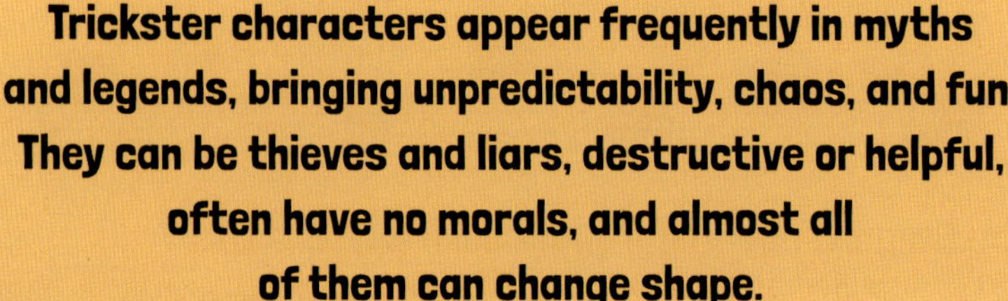

Trickster characters appear frequently in myths and legends, bringing unpredictability, chaos, and fun. They can be thieves and liars, destructive or helpful, often have no morals, and almost all of them can change shape.

Coyote

The story of Coyote is told by many Indigenous American peoples. He is usually male and human-shaped, although he can have fur, pointy ears, a tail, yellow eyes, and claws like a wild **coyote** dog. Coyote is both cunning and thoughtless, does harm and good, and doesn't care about right and wrong. **He can even play tricks on himself.**

In one White River **Sioux** story, Coyote and his trickster friend Iktome the Spider-man found a storytelling rock called Iya. Coyote gave Iya his beautiful blanket, but when the weather became stormy, he took it back again.

Iya was offended, and although Coyote thought he'd got away with it, he hadn't. After the storm passed, the great rock suddenly came hurtling straight at Coyote and Iktome. They ran for it and then swam across a river, but the rolling stone just kept coming, smashing down the trees in its way. Iktome changed himself into his spider form and scurried down a hole, but Iya caught Coyote, squashed him flat like a rug, and took the blanket.

Some time later, a man came past and thought Coyote really was a rug, and took him home. However, the next morning the "new rug" **ran away.**

Coyote could always come back to life.

Speak like a mythologist

METAMORPHOSIS

Metamorphosis means the change of something or someone into a completely different form. Many tales of supernatural transformation are told by the ancient Roman poet Ovid in a poem called the *Metamorphoses*, published about 8 CE. Ovid is one of the most popular authors about myth in European literature.

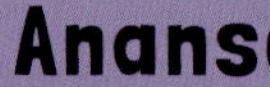

Ananse

Ashanti people of West Africa have a tale in which the sky god Nyame owned all the stories and knowledge. The trickster, Ananse the Spider, wanted to buy this information. Nyame would sell it in return for the Python, the Leopard, the Hornets, and a **Fairy.**

Ananse found the Python. "I wonder whether the Python is longer than a palm branch," he said. The snake

stretched out, offering to be measured, and Ananse tied him to the palm branch and delivered him to Nyame. Next Ananse dug a hole and covered it over with leaves. When the Leopard fell into the trap, Ananse pretended to help him, but tangled up the Leopard in his spiderweb, and then the Leopard was hauled off to Nyame too.

There are many different interpretations of how Ananse looks.

Ananse caught the Hornets by creating a pretend rain shower and offering to keep them safe in his **gourd.** When they flew into it, he plugged up the hole and carried them back to Nyame. Finally, Ananse made a wooden doll covered with sticky gum, and put some **yams** in its hands. One of the Fairies ate some of the yams, but ended up stuck to the gum, and Ananse carried the captured Fairy to Nyame.

Nyame was impressed and gave Ananse the stories. Ananse put all the world's wisdom into his gourd, but **accidentally** broke it, and so everyone in the world was able to share the knowledge.

Loki

The Marvel character Loki, **god of mischief,** was inspired by the Norse trickster god Loki, who could change shape and gender at will. Norse Loki became a fly, a salmon, and a mare that gave birth to an eight-legged wonder-horse called Sleipnir.

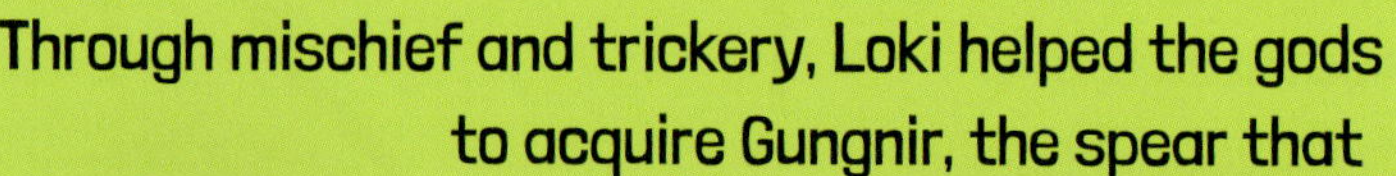

Through mischief and trickery, Loki helped the gods to acquire Gungnir, the spear that never missed its target, Skidbladnir, the ship that could carry all the gods but could be folded up into a pocket, and Thor's hammer, Mjölnir.

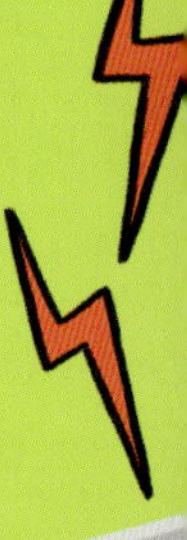

Loki was charming and funny, but they were also a cunning, cowardly, selfish liar, and was jealous of Odin and Frigg's popular son Baldur. When Baldur had dreams that prophesied his own death, Frigg made every living thing promise not to harm him,

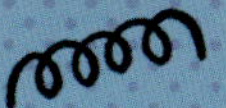

but overlooked the mistletoe plant. When the gods played a silly game where they threw things at Baldur without harming him, Loki tricked the god Hod into hurling a mistletoe spear, which hit Baldur and killed him instantly.

Hel, goddess of the underworld, agreed to release Baldur if everyone would weep for him. Everyone did, apart from the cold-hearted Tokk, who was actually Loki. So Baldur had to stay in the underworld, but the gods took vengeance for Loki's many crimes. They used the entrails of his son, Narfi, to tie him to a rock underneath the jaws of a serpent that dripped venom on to his face, causing earthquakes as **he writhed in agony.**

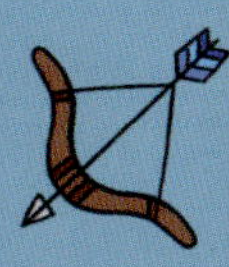

HEROES OF MYTH AND LEGEND

THOR

The thunder god of Norse mythology who rode across the sky in a goat-drawn chariot. His most famous possession was his hammer, Mjölnir, which means "Lightning."

Māui

In the culture of the **Polynesian** Islanders, Māui is a cunning trickster. Tales about him were told for hundreds of years, and first recorded around 130 years ago.

The Islanders tell many different stories about Māui. In some of them he created the islands of Hawaii and New Zealand by fishing them out of the sea using a magic fishhook made from his grandmother's jawbone.

There are also amazing stories about how, in order to steal fire from the gods, he recited a poem that opened the gateway to the underworld, and then shrank himself and hid inside a red pigeon, which flew to the fire god Mauike.

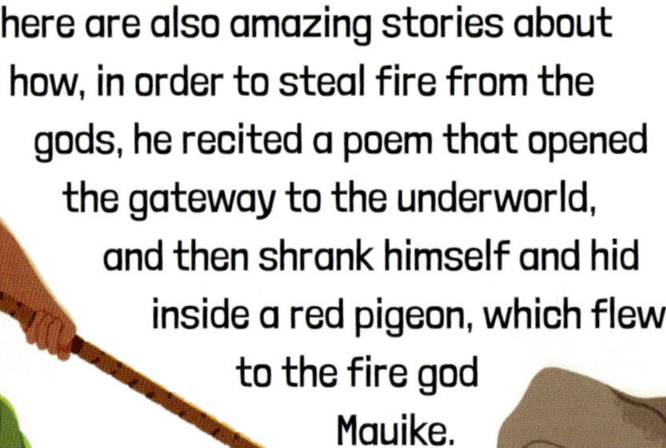

Back in human shape, Māui won a fight with Mauike, and made the god teach him how to make fire. He grabbed two fire-sticks, hid inside the pigeon, and flew back to the upper world, where he shared the secret of fire with humans.

The days were too short because the sun god Tama-nui-te-rā moved across the sky too quickly. So, Māui captured Tama-nui-te-rā and threatened him with the enchanted jawbone until he promised to move more slowly.

Finally, Māui tried to win eternal life from the death-goddess Hine-nui-te-pō, but she crushed him to death. Māui still lives on in stories and in the Disney film *Moana*, where Moana, a chief's daughter, meets him in her quest to save her people.

Tricksters often use their powers to try to help humans, as well as playing tricks on them. Because they break rules, they often get into fights with the gods. But as we are about to discover, there were other mighty conflicts involving gods, heroes, and humans that were fought in stories all across the world.

Chapter 8

Mythical Wars

War stories are always compelling, and the legendary battles of gods vs. gods, heroes vs. heroes, gods vs. mortals, or Good vs. Evil are some of the best ever told.

Indra vs. Vritra

The *Rig Veda*, the ancient Hindu scriptures, are written in **Sanskrit** and date from about 1500 BCE. They tell of how Indra, king of the gods, faced a gigantic challenge from the serpent-dragon-demon Vritra. The monster had coiled himself round a mountain, built ninety-nine fortresses, and blocked up the rivers, causing a terrible drought. So, Indra went to Tvastar, the maker

Vritra

of divine weapons, who created the *vajra*, which was as indestructible as diamonds and as irresistible as thunderbolts.

Indra fortified himself by drinking three sacred beakers of *soma*, the plant juice of immortality, and stormed into battle. Vritra collapsed under Indra's onslaught and crushed all the fortresses as he fell. The dragon still fought on, though, until Indra finally smashed him between the shoulders with his *vajra*. As Vritra lay in lifeless pieces, Indra set the rivers free, and their waters rushed down like bellowing cows. Indra then gave life to the Sun, dawn, and heaven, and slew Vritra's mother Danu, bringing order to the world and earning the title of The Great Impetuous Many-Slaying Hero.

Troy

The story of the Trojan War is about a conflict between heroes, although the **Olympian gods and goddesses** also joined in. The story sounds like a real war, and some people think it might have really happened.

Speak like a mythologist

THE *ILIAD*

Homer's *Iliad* is an epic poem telling the story of the Trojan War and the hero Achilles, who was disrespected, sulked, lost his best friend, and killed his worst enemy. In the end he realized that there was more to life than revenge, and more to adulthood than slaughtering other people.

Trojan prince Paris was made to decide which goddess should be given a golden apple bearing the words "for the fairest."

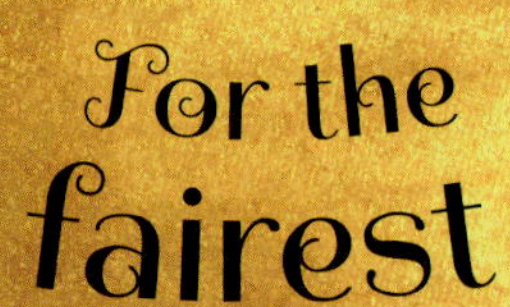

He chose Aphrodite because she promised him Helen, the most **beautiful** woman on Earth, and the war began when Paris kidnapped Helen, who was already married to Menelaus.

The Greeks sent an army on a fleet of 1,106 ships to get Helen back. Their best fighter and ***fastest runner*** was Achilles. His goddess mother wanted to make him immortal, so she dipped him in the **River Styx** as a baby, making him totally invulnerable everywhere except for his heel, where she had held him.

At Troy, the Trojan warrior Hector slew Achilles' best friend Patroclus (some scholars think that Achilles and Patroclus were lovers). Achilles knew about a prophecy that he would die if he rejoined the battle, but he didn't care. He went into battle, fought against a river god, and drove all the Trojans except Hector inside their city.

Hector tried to run for safety, but Achilles chased him three times around Troy's walls before slaying him. True to the prophecy, Achilles was killed soon after by an arrow that struck him in his heel.

With Greece's finest fighter lost, another warrior, cunning Odysseus, had the idea of building a **huge wooden horse.** The Greek army pretended to sail away, and despite being told to "beware of Greeks bearing gifts," the curious Trojans dragged the horse into their city to see what this mysterious present was.

Greek warriors hiding inside it jumped out and opened the city gates to let in the waiting Greek army.

The Greek army burned Troy to the ground, massacred the men, enslaved the women and children, and sailed home with Helen.

ACHILLES

Ancient Greek hero. Achilles was given the choice between a long but unremarkable life or a short, glorious one. He chose glory. Because of the way he died, some people now use "Achilles heel" to describe a vulnerable point or a weakness. In your body, the Achilles tendon connects your calf muscles to your heel bone.

Emperor Huang Di vs. Chiyou

One of the **most famous** figures in Chinese mythology and culture is Huang Di, who was honest, clever, and wise. He lived to be **300** years old.

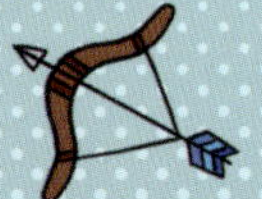

Huang Di was challenged by Chiyou, a creature who had eighty brothers with animal bodies, bronze heads, iron brows, and who ate sand and stone. Chiyou was also a blacksmith. He made weapons and attacked Huang Di with an army of fierce creatures on the plain of **Zhuolu**.

Both sides used magic, and when Chiyou enveloped the battlefield in supernatural fog, Huang Di's warriors made their way through the mist using Fang, a miraculous south-pointing chariot that had a wooden person with a magnetic hand fixed to it.

Huang Di ordered the dragon Yinglong to battle with Chiyou, but when the dragon gathered up all the water, Chiyou unleashed Feng Po, the hideous Wind Master, and the Rain Master, Yu Shih.

Huang Di called on his daughter, Ba the Drought-Ghoul, to descend, and she stopped the wind and rain. Eventually Chiyou was killed, and Huang Di was carried up to heaven on a dragon and became a god.

The **Han** people, who make up about 90% of China's population and 19% of the world's population, are still seen as the descendants of Huang Di.

Huang Di

The great mythological wars could cause destruction to humankind, but so could natural disasters. As we shall see in the next chapter, the gods could attack humans with devastating floods.

Chapter 9

Flood Myths

All over the world there are tales about a Great Flood. Even though there probably never was one enormous cataclysm, the details of these stories can be amazingly similar.

There is often conflict between the gods and humans in which nearly all mortals are destroyed, but sometimes humans are given a second chance and bounce back stronger than before.

Noah, Atrahasis, and Ut-napishtim

In the Jewish and Christian Bible story of the Great Flood, God told Noah to build a **large** ship known as the Ark. Noah and his family and pairs of different animals went aboard the Ark and were saved from the flood.

They knew the world was drying out when a dove Noah sent out returned with an olive leaf, and then finally didn't return at all.

There are similar tales in the **Mesopotamian** *Epic of Atrahasis* and the Babylonian *Epic of Gilgamesh*, in which the heroes Atrahasis and Ut-napishtim tell how they survived the flood.

In the *Epic of Atrahasis*, the gods sent the flood because humans were too noisy. In both stories one of the gods warned the hero, telling him to build a boat, abandon possessions, and save lives. So, Atrahasis and Ut-napishtim both built

enormous

cube-shaped boats and sailed off on them with their families and various animals.

The gods sent down showers of bread, wheat, birds, and fish, and then started a countdown to the deluge on a water clock.

Speak like a mythologist

THE *EPIC OF GILGAMESH*

The Babylonian *Epic of Gilgamesh* was composed around 1100 BCE and survives on twelve clay cuneiform tablets in the Akkadian language. It is about the adventures of the young King Gilgamesh who is seeking immortality. When Ut-napishtim tells him this is impossible, Gilgamesh focuses on becoming a good king instead.

As the weather got worse the storm gods **roared,** the boats started to float, the sky was torn apart, the land was smashed like a broken pot, and everything went dark. Even the gods themselves were frightened by what had happened. The storm lasted seven days.

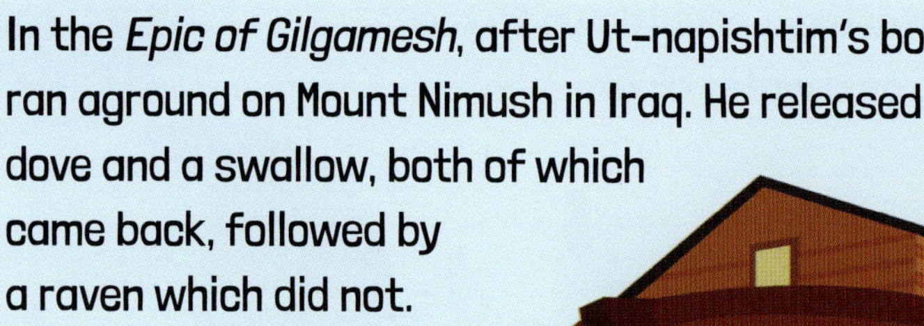

In the *Epic of Gilgamesh*, after Ut-napishtim's boat ran aground on Mount Nimush in Iraq. He released a dove and a swallow, both of which came back, followed by a raven which did not.

Speak like a mythologist

THE *EPIC OF ATRAHASIS*

The Mesopotamian *Epic of Atrahasis* was written down during the reign of King Ammisaduqa of Babylonia around 1600 BCE. It contains a creation myth and a flood myth that probably influenced the story of Noah.

Then he made a sacrifice to the gods, and the weather god Enlil decreed that Ut-napishtim and his wife should become like the gods.

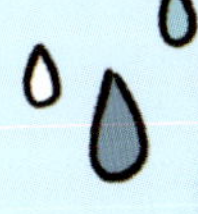

In the *Epic of Atrahasis* the gods got hungry because there were no more farmers, and no one was sacrificing any more. They realized that they needed human beings, so when they discovered that Atrahasis had survived, they decided that the human noise was okay within limits, but made sure that not too many humans would be born in future.

Plato's Atlantis

In works called *Timaeus* and *Critias*, from the fourth century BCE, Greek philosopher Plato invented an amazing flood myth about the island of Atlantis, which was in the Atlantic Ocean and seemed like a wondrous paradise. The wealth of its kings was **astonishing,** every kind of animal lived there, the cities were exquisite, and the earth produced everything they could ever wish for.

But Atlanteans still wanted more. After they tried and failed to conquer the city of Athens, Zeus punished them with a **cataclysmic** natural disaster. Atlantis disappeared under water in one awful day and night.

Plato's message in the story is, "Keep it simple and modest, don't ask more for than you need, and don't be like those imaginary Atlanteans because it will only end badly." Did Atlantis ever really exist? It was certainly just a story with a moral, although that has not stopped people searching for Atlantis ever since.

Speak like a mythologist

CATACLYSM

The floods are literally cataclysmic! The ancient Greek word *kataklysmos* means "flood."

None of these Great Floods destroyed the whole of humanity. All the ghosts of the people who were drowned in these terrible events were believed to go

down to the underworld,

but the survivors were all given a second chance. And as we are about to find out . . . the underworld was a strange place, and there were other ways in which the end of the world would come.

Chapter 10

The Underworld and the End of the World

Most mythologies divide the Universe into three levels: the heavens, where the gods live; the earth, inhabited by humans; and an underworld, sometimes known as hell.

Different cultures have diverse ideas about life after death, and about how the world itself might end. Some people see time as a straight line, with a beginning and end, while others see it as cycles of creation and destruction, with each cycle ending in an apocalyptic battle or natural disaster.

Speak like a mythologist

APOCALYPSE

Today we use "apocalypse" to mean an event that causes destruction on a massive scale, and "Armageddon" for a terrible conflict that could wipe out humans. In the Christian Bible the *Book of Revelation* (aka The Apocalypse) tells the final battle between the forces of Good and Evil will be fought at a place called Armageddon in ancient Palestine.

Duat, the Egyptian underworld

The ancient Egyptians believed that there was a vast underworld, the *Duat*, beneath the earth. The *Duat* was ruled by the god Osiris, and every night the sun god Ra would sail through it on his night boat, the *Mesektet*, and be reborn in the morning.

The dead made a similar journey and had to get past gods, mysterious creatures, and demon gatekeepers, although they had *The Book of the Dead* to guide them, and the jackal-headed god Anubis made sure they didn't get lost.

When they reached the Hall of Judgment, the dead had to appear in front of forty-two divine judges. *The Book of the Dead* helped them to say all the right things, even if they were not totally innocent. But then came the "Weighing of the Heart."

Everybody's heart recorded everything they had ever done. So, it was placed on one side of a balance, with a single feather of Ma'at, the winged goddess of truth, on the other.

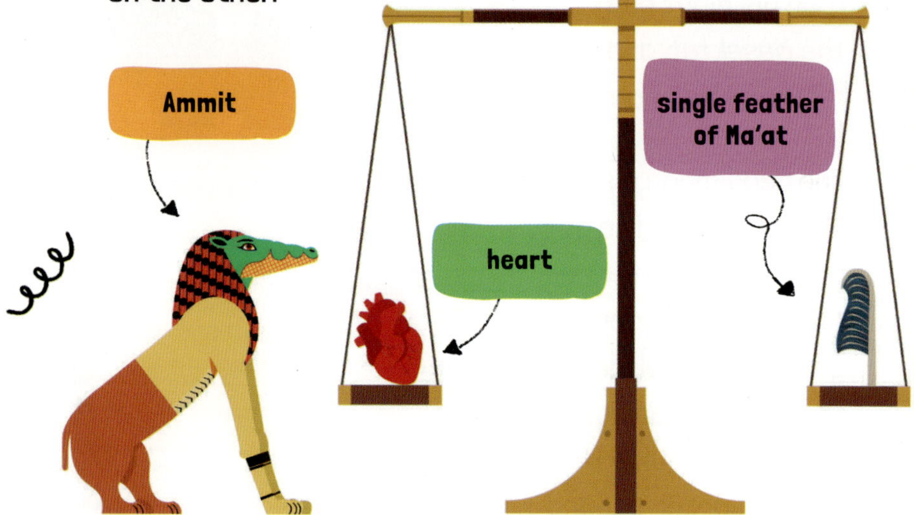

If the heart weighed more than the feather, it was fed to Ammit, a demon who was part hippopotamus, part wild cat, and part crocodile, and the dead person would simply disappear forever. But if the scales balanced, they had passed the test, and Osiris would welcome them into the afterlife.

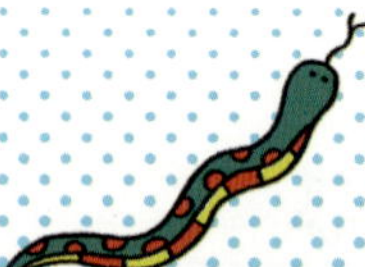

EGYPTIAN *BOOK OF THE DEAD*

The Book of Coming Forth by Day, also known as *The Book of the Dead*, is actually a huge collection of spells. The spells were usually written on a papyrus roll that was placed with the dead person, but sometimes they were inscribed or painted on the walls of their tomb.

Details of the ancient *The Book of Coming Forth by Day*, also known as *The Book of the Dead*, (1070 BCE), Thebes, Egypt

Milu, Hiku, and Kawelu: the Hawaiian underworld

The Hawaiian chief Milu became god of the underworld, known as Lua-o-Milu, after he disappeared in a surfing accident. In his kingdom under the sea, he organized sports and games like the ones that his ghostly subjects enjoyed when they were alive.

In a Hawaiian legend recorded in the nineteenth century, Hiku and Kawelu were a newly married couple. They had a terrible argument and Kawelu ended her own life leaving Hiku heartbroken. Hiku decided to go to Lua-o-Milu to bring Kawelu back from the dead. To get to the underworld, a priest told him, he must paddle his canoe into the middle of the ocean and let down one end of a vine into the water.

Hiku did as he was told and climbed down the vine into the underworld. He began to swing on the vine, and the spirits all jumped on to play on it too. Even Milu joined in. Eventually, Kawelu's ghost joined in the game, and straight away Hiku called to the people on his canoe to pull up the vine, while he held on tightly to Kawelu.

Hiku brought Kawelu to their home, where her dead body lay. He pushed her spirit back into her body from the feet upward, and Kawelu crowed like a cockerel and was restored to life. She and Hiku went back to living as husband and wife.

Milu, god of the underworld

Mictlan

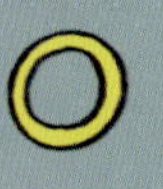

The people of the Aztec Empire, who lived in what's now Mexico, believed that there were thirteen levels in the heavens and nine in the underworld, which was called Mictlan.

In Aztec mythology, unlike the myths of ancient Egypt and Greece, what happened to people after death did not depend on how they had lived, but on the way they died. Warriors and women who died in childbirth went to the land of the sun god Tonatiuh; those who died by drowning, certain diseases, or being hit by lightning went to the mansion of the rain god Tlaloc; but adults who died of other causes went to Mictlan and young children went to Xoxchatlalpan (place of abundance and flowers).

The descent through the nine levels included passing through the Place of the Obsidian-bladed Winds, where the air cut their skin like a knife, the Place Where People are Killed by Arrows, and the Place Where People's Hearts are Devoured.

Finally, they reached the Place That has No Outlet for Smoke, and met the Lord and Lady of Death, Mictlantecuhtli and Mictecacihuatl, who fed on a diet of feet, hands, **beetle stew,** and a **porridge made of pus** that they drank from skulls.

Mictlantecuhtli wore a headdress of owl feathers, a necklace of **human eyeballs**, and his clawed hands carried a knife to remove people's hearts.

Mictlan was the place of ultimate disappearance, but there is no record of how the Aztecs believed the dead spent the rest of time.

Ragnarök

In the Norse *Prose Edda*, the end of the world is Ragnarök. Three severe winters, full of war, will be followed by The Great Winter, which will engulf the world in ice for three years. The wolves Sköll and Hati will swallow the Sun and Moon, and earthquakes will rock the earth. Loki and his son, the terrifying wolf Fenrir, will break their chains and Hel's guard dog Garm will snap the rope that tethers him.

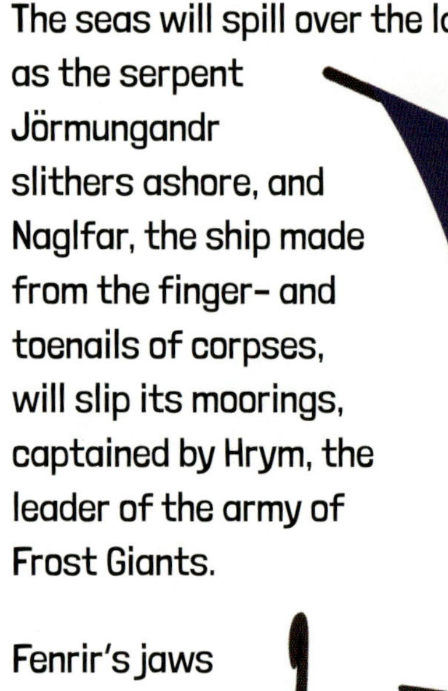

The seas will spill over the land as the serpent Jörmungandr slithers ashore, and Naglfar, the ship made from the finger- and toenails of corpses, will slip its moorings, captained by Hrym, the leader of the army of Frost Giants.

Hrym captaining the ship Naglfar

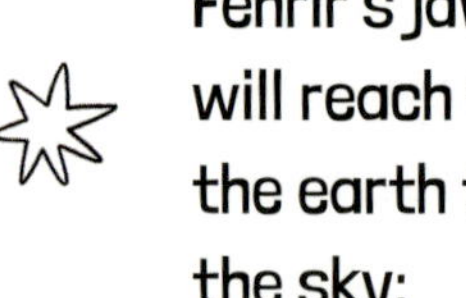

Fenrir's jaws will reach from the earth to the sky;

Jörmungandr will belch poison; Surt, the leader of the Fire Giants, will lead them across the Rainbow Bridge between the earth and the sky, and it will shatter beneath them. After Asgard's guardian Hiemdall has summoned the gods with the loud-sounding horn called the Gjallarhorn, Odin will ride to the Well of Knowledge to seek advice, and the cosmic tree Yggdrasil will tremble. The gods will march from Odin's heavenly hall of **Valhalla**, and battle will be joined on the field of Vígrid.

Odin, in golden armor and wielding his magical spear Gungnir, will duel with Fenrir, but the wolf will swallow him. Thor will slay Jörmungandr but die from the serpent's venom. Freyr, the god "hated by none," will lose to Surt. Garm and the war god Tyr will kill each other, and so will Loki and Hiemdall. Odin's son Vidar will kick Fenrir's jaws open with his **magic shoe** and thrust his sword into his heart.

Finally, Surt will send fire through all the Nine Worlds, putting an end to humans, gods and goddesses, giants, **elves**, and **dwarves**, before the world sinks beneath the waters. However, in the *Poetic Edda* this is not the end of the story. Baldur will eventually lead a number of gods back to Asgard, and a new green, bright, fertile world will emerge from the waves.

Chapter 11

Myths, Legends, and Superheroes in the Modern World

These myths and legends are hundreds, sometimes thousands, of years old, but there is no sign of them fading away. The exciting plots and fascinating characters in these enchanting and inspiring stories still entrance us with their magic.

We can travel back in time on our own journeys of discovery, sail the Seven Seas with Sindbad, watch the world come into being, and rid it of dangerous and mysterious creatures. And we can see the ancient characters morphing into today's superheroes, as the Norse Thor wields his magic hammer Mjölnir in the **Marvel Universe**, the Amazon Wonder Woman saves the world from chaos and destruction, and Percy Jackson traverses a gloriously reimagined world of Greek gods and goddesses.

We can find our own special hidden meanings in these stories too, although these won't be the same for all of us because myths and legends speak to everyone in different ways. They can be totally illogical, and yet they make perfect sense. They are full of truth. They change all the time, but they are fixed forever. And they explain things that can't really be explained.

Glossary

Allah Arabic word for God among Muslims

Anglo-Saxon earliest recorded form of the English language, spoken in England and parts of Scotland in around 450–1150 CE

Babylon rich and powerful ancient city on the River Euphrates in what is now Iraq

BCE stands for "before common era"

Buddha Siddartha Gautama, the "awakened" or "enlightened" one, who renounced his wealth and family and taught everybody who came to learn from him. He founded the religion or philosophy called Buddhism

CE stands for "common era"

Christian Bible "Christian" is the name originally given by the Greeks and Romans to the followers of Jesus. The Bible is the sacred writings of the Christian religion

coyote North American wild dog, similar to but smaller than a wolf

cuneiform very early writing system that uses wedge-shaped characters

DC Comics one of the oldest American comic book publishers. The imaginary DC Universe features superheroes such as Superman, Wonder Woman, and Batman

diaspora people who have been dispersed from their homeland

divine like a god or goddess

druid Celtic ancient priest, magician, wizard, or soothsayer

dwarves mythical Norse creatures. They live underground, and are brilliant blacksmiths and craftspeople

elves god-like beings in Norse mythology who are more beautiful than the Sun

epic long poem about the exploits of legendary heroic characters

ethnographer a person who studies and describes the customs and behavior of human cultures, often using first-hand observation and interviews

fairy supernatural being in human form, usually represented as small, clever, and playful, with magical powers

Geatland Beowulf's kingdom in what is now southern Sweden

gourd hard-shelled fruit that can be dried and used to make containers and other useful objects

Greek mythology the group of stories about gods, goddesses, heroes, and creatures of ancient Greece. These are some of the most well-known and long-lasting tales in the world

Han the largest ethnic group in China

Islam related to the Muslim religion. In Arabic "Islam" means submission to the will of God

K'iche' Maya people who flourished in Mexico and Central America between about 300 and 900 CE.

Marvel Universe a modern fictional universe produced by Marvel Comics and Marvel Studios that is full of characters with superhuman powers, who are dedicated to protecting humanity

mermaid a mythical creature with the upper body of a woman and the tail of a fish

Mesopotamia the ancient region between the Tigris and Euphrates Rivers, now in Iraq. Mesopotamia means "the place between the rivers"

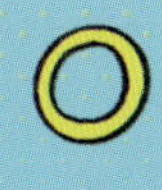

Norse a word that describes the ancient Norwegians and Scandinavians and their language and culture

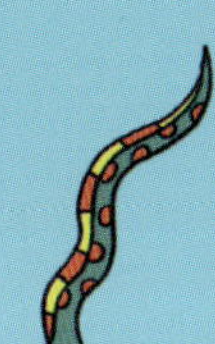

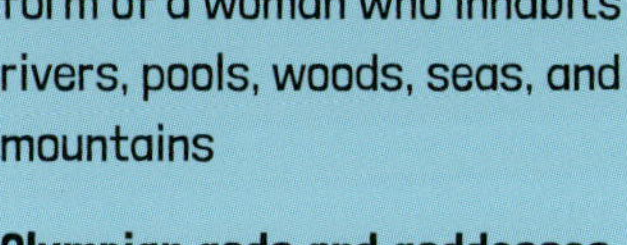

nymph a spirit of nature in the form of a woman who inhabits rivers, pools, woods, seas, and mountains

Olympian gods and goddesses Zeus, Hera, Poseidon, Apollo, Artemis, Athena, Aphrodite, Hephaestus, Dionysus, Hermes, Ares, and Demeter—the Greek divinities whose home is on Mount Olympus in Greece

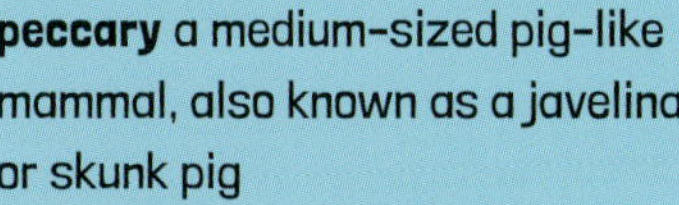

peccary a medium-sized pig-like mammal, also known as a javelina or skunk pig

Poetic Edda collection of anonymous poems from the eighth to eleventh centuries that records many tales of Norse mythology

Polynesia an area of islands between Hawaii, New Zealand, and Easter Island in the Central and South Pacific Ocean

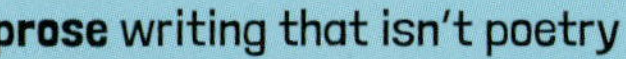

prose writing that isn't poetry

Prose Edda Norse textbook written in Iceland during the early thirteenth century by a scholar called Snorri Sturluson

quest long or difficult search for something or someone

River Styx mythical river that divides the earth from the underworld

saga long story of heroic deeds, especially one told in Old Norse or Old Icelandic

Sanskrit the ancient language of South Asia, and the sacred language of Hinduism

Sioux an alliance of tribes of Indigenous American peoples from the South and Midwest USA

Sirens musical enchanters who bewitched sailors and lured them to their deaths

Thebes important city in central Greece that featured in many Greek myths. Not to be confused Thebes on the River Nile, the capital of the kingdom of Egypt in its heyday

Trojan War mythical ten-year siege of Troy by the Greeks after the Trojan prince Paris kidnapped Helen from her husband Menelaus

Tupí-Guaraní South American peoples who mainly inhabit rainforest areas around the River Amazon

Valhalla great hall ruled by Norse god Odin, where warriors go if they have died fighting

Valkyrie attendants of Norse god Odin. They decide the outcomes of battles and take the souls of slain warriors to Valhalla

yam vegetable that you can boil and mash, or fry, roast, or bake, common in West African countries

Zhuolu region of northern China

zither musical instrument played with the fingers and a plectrum. It has a flat wooden sound box with about forty strings stretched across it

Index

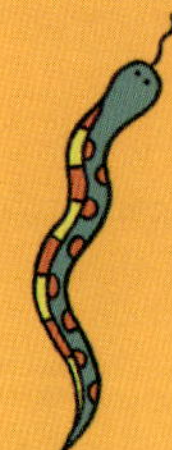

Introducing the Myths and Legends experts:

AUTHOR

DR. STEPHEN KERSHAW

Dr. Stephen Kershaw is the tutor of Oxford University's Greek Mythology: Online course. His publications on mythology include *The Penguin Dictionary of Classical Mythology*, *A Brief Guide to Greek Mythology*, and *Mythologica*, which was Amazon's Best Children's Non-Fiction Book of 2019. He lives in Oxfordshire with his wife and a spaniel called Hero.

CONSULTANT

DR. SILVIE KILGALLON

Dr. Silvie Kilgallon completed a PhD in Classics at the University of Bristol, focusing on the works of the ancient Greek poet Hesiod. She now lives in Germany, with another human and three cats, and researches magical texts in the ancient world.

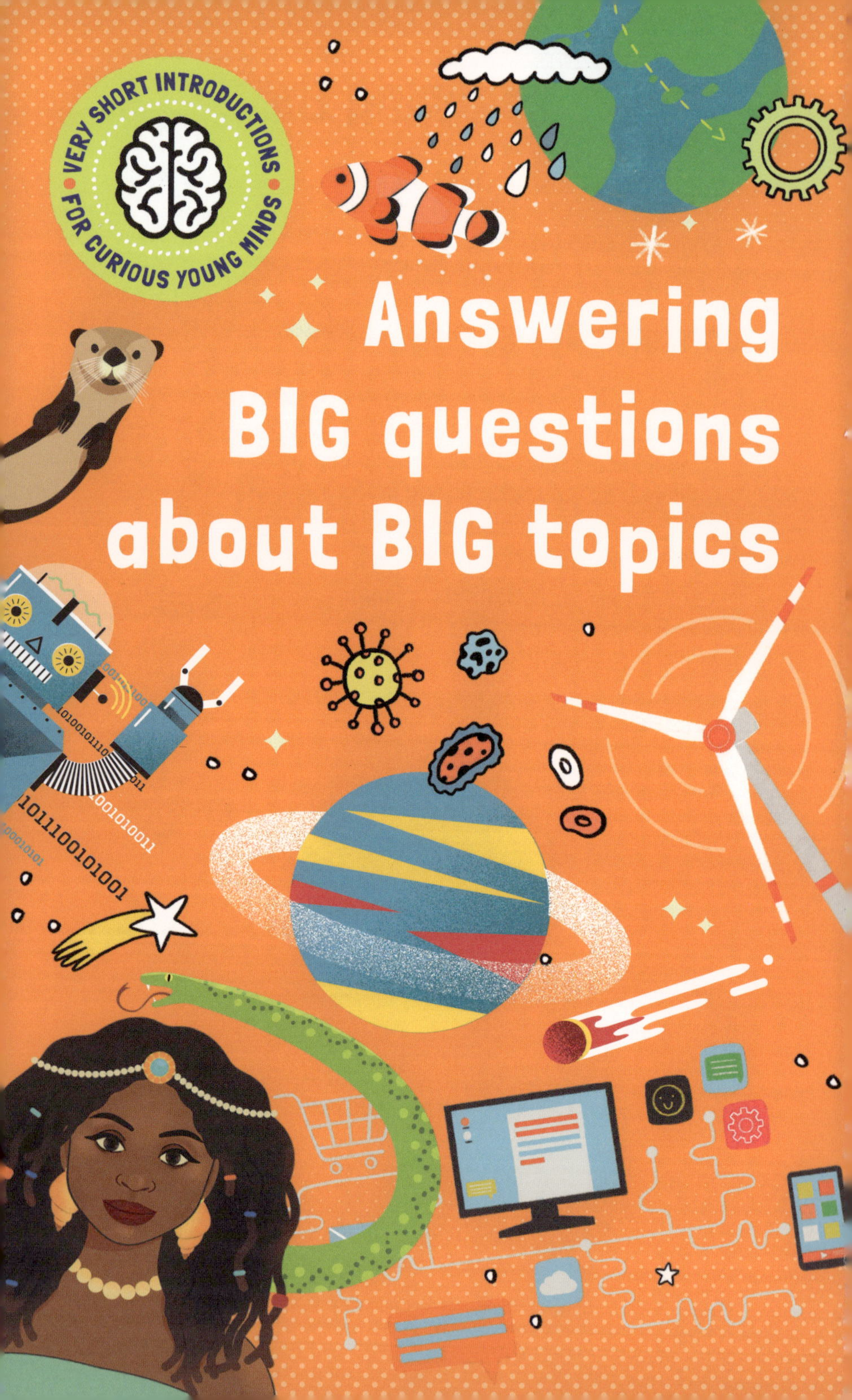
VERY SHORT INTRODUCTIONS
FOR CURIOUS YOUNG MINDS
Answering
BIG questions
about BIG topics